## About the Author

Jimmy Watkins is a British author releasing his debut collection of poetry. He is based in the New Forest, Hampshire where much of his inspiration stems from.

# THROES OF WINTER

JIMMY WATKINS

---

**THROES OF WINTER**

Vanguard Press

VANGUARD PAPERBACK

© Copyright 2023
**Jimmy Watkins**

The right of Jimmy Watkins to be identified as author of
this work has been asserted by him in accordance with the
Copyright, Designs and Patents Act 1988.

**All Rights Reserved**

No reproduction, copy or transmission of this publication
may be made without written permission.
No paragraph of this publication may be reproduced,
copied or transmitted save with the written permission of the
publisher, or in accordance with the provisions
of the Copyright Act 1956 (as amended).

Any person who commits any unauthorised act in relation to
this publication may be liable to criminal
prosecution and civil claims for damages.

A CIP catalogue record for this title is
available from the British Library.

ISBN 978-1-80016-806-0

*Vanguard Press is an imprint of
Pegasus Elliot Mackenzie Publishers Ltd.*
www.pegasuspublishers.com

First Published in 2023

**Vanguard Press
Sheraton House Castle Park
Cambridge England**

Printed & Bound in Great Britain

# Dedication

To friends and family, whose support allowed me to find my truest self. To Tracey and Ivy, who laid the foundations for my love of language. To LCS, your love gave me the power to explore new worlds. Your light filled lanterns that lead me home.

# Acknowledgements

I would like to issue my sincere thanks to all those who gave such valuable feedback on my work. You took the time to consider the meaning of every word, and I shall be forever grateful for it. Immense gratitude must be given to all those who give their time and energy to help maintain public gardens and National Parks. They allow us to explore the beauty of this land and marvel at the colours and sounds in all their glory.

# Table of Contents

**NATURE'S LESSONS**
Howling Dawn
Their Courage
A Ferry's Fight
Hope of Spring
Belladona
Raptures of a River
Sing and Glide
Ode to Lady's Slipper

**PERSONAL EXPRESSIONS**
Tenebrous Steps
Sobriety
Desperate Voice
Shouldering Regrets
Solace on a Page
Knowledge or Hope?
The Might of the Pen

**HISTORICAL SUPPRESSIONS**
Unquiet Civility
Castle by the Sea
The Final Quest
Forbidden Binding
Song of The Inn
Ode to Tennyson
A Friendly Game

**TIMELESS CONNECTIONS**
Winter's Widow
The Writer all at Sea
In-between Worlds
Pestilence of Pretence
Sharing the Seasons
Clear the Canvas
Seeking Commonality
When Christmas Stopped

## Howling Dawn

Bring forth waves that crash the lurid shore,
Hold your posture, still and sure.
Embrace the crashing at thy door,
Nebulous and yet, sensed before.

Bring forth the driving rain upon the lawn,
Release your limbs upon this dawn.
Embrace the sounds that feel forlorn,
Shrouded and yet, ne'er withdrawn.

Yield to the biting wind as it prowls,
Bow your head as temper growls.
See the rayless face as it scowls,
Stygian and yet, its beauty howls.

Yield to the love of all that's grey,
Kneel to the waves that show the way.
See all in wonder, let it portray,
Obscure and yet, felt this day.

# Their Courage

The Summer Solstice has long since gone,
Even the fall has insidiously withdrawn.
Drop by drop; as the moisture cools,
Creatures of the forest hath become nature's fools.
The bitterness of the night; bites at the dormouse,
They lack the guile of the playful grouse.
Nocturnal heroes strive to build their nest,
So their babies can avoid an eternal rest.
Bats seek their roost when the snap sets in,
Dreaming of unfettered flights to begin.
Can we preserve their habitat; for when solace goes,
Or aid their battle against wintry throes?

Some suffer less as they fall into torpor,
But survival still requires they be a great hoarder.
Strenuous and suffocating; the enemy is still there,
Badgers must wait for their moment to dare.
'Roam the leaves and make it count,
Ne'er let the army steal your mount.'
Should squirrels desire to leave their abode,
Courage is needed to receive what they're owed.
From dusk to dawn; they all face this fight,

Huddled on the precipice until Spring is in sight.
Faced with the instinct that compels us to shield,
Would we show their verve and never yield?

# A Ferry's Fight

Show me where the vastness of life opens wide,
That place where the mouth is hungry but always brim-full.
Hold my hand in the face of a sardonic tide,
And kiss me softly in waves so playful.
The hydrous heart perdures most powerful.

Shield me from the capacious mist that looms,
Engulfing the air in a frenzied motion.
Steady my feet when thine engine booms,
Whisper urbanely to quieten the ocean.
Point me to a calming pillar should Poseidon take a notion.

Carry the souls starting their journey home,
Comfort them when shadows begin to lengthen.
Fight against the barrage of fear and foam,
Caress the wheel once the forces strengthen.
Try to dent their spirit to frighten.

Should you emerge through the eye of the storm,
Your efforts must not cease; as skirmishes still remain.
Be wary of the insurgence in aqueous form,
It will strike the hull should sight go again.
Your passengers are anchored; awaiting a peaceful domain.

Know your path that sought the harbour,
Stars were lanterns that lit the way.
Be gracious when sojourns sing much calmer,
They'll still need steel should barriers block the bay.
Your passengers are ashore, appreciating your will today.

# Hope of Spring

Oft we wonder this trail entwine,
Past the Norman church in shrine.
Hands held like solid vine,
With ripened assurance, that I am thine.

Oft we see the sun ahead,
'Between the ancient trees', you said.
Hands pulsating each step we tread,
With blooming affection, our love is spread.

Yet, tomorrow I fear that you'll be gone,
An emptiness shall grow where light had shone.
Broken branches we can't rely on,
Telling of dubiety in things anon.

Yet if I wish to allay this fear,
I can't be afraid to shed a tear.
Broken voices sound in my ear,
Telling of hope, may I not veer.

# Belladona

Blinded in a chasm of loves' thorny throes,
I thrash at spectres where Bella grows.
Ne'er has she sung so sweet before,
Beckoning me to kiss her venomous core.
My flesh tingles in wake of your power,
Removing the pain from my most lonely hour.
O' love! Guide my lips to thee,
Bring forth sultry waves to carry me.

Deafened by sounds that lead me astray,
Abounding branches push me away.
Yet, I must pull free and touch your flower,
My tongue is loose and ready to devour.
Remove my memories that are dark and binding,
Your noxious nectar; stops my heart from fighting.
You are suspended in time; though age has passed,
An ephemeral existence cannot last.

## Raptures of a River

Resplendent rivers roam the land,
Saliently shifting nature's strand.
When banks oppressively overflow,
Fresh wild wonders of life will show.
Fear not; the creatures of the sky,
You'll still spot prey from up high.
The source of hope is in each drop,
A ribbon of life that cannot stop.
The source of dreams cures the crop,
Enchanting fauna from tail to top.
You'll rest for now with a languid sigh,
Fear not; the spell will pass on by.
Laden with love from mother's bow,
When algae begin to graciously glow.
Sedentary shadows will be on hand,
Revealing raptures for life to expand.

## Sing and Glide

Sing sweetheart; should you sense the stage,
Provide pleasure and poise on every page.
Rhythm rumbles rarefied amongst the raucous rally,
Intensely intimate and imaginative, felt instantly.
Ne'er name negative noise as it's nothing new,
Glide graciously goddess, in the garden you grew.

# Ode to Lady's Slipper

Amongst the fauna of the Yorkshire Dales,
Rests a lady with haunting tales.
Elegantly she sings in bloom;
For 'tis thirteen years she hath stood alone,
The nation had whispered of her kind no more.
Yet, out of 'extinction'; a spirit did loom,
A spectral symmetry burst out from the gloom.
Through 'Victorian Delirium' the Slipper prevails.
All hunters and collectors; you must beware,
Mischievous traps are laid to halt you.
Each is designed to keep her safe,
So, none can know from whence she grew.

One single flower is fused into a single column,
Unlike those who enviously watch her blossom.
Proudly fibrous in golden yellow;
Awaiting her keepers to tend to her needs,
For once blossomed this be her only life.
The lady's protectors guard her with faces mellow,
Hands are withered from tending to her below.
Her voice hath reached us; united we stand solemn.
All hunters and collectors; you must beware,

Mischievous traps are laid to halt you.
Each is designed to keep her safe,
So, none can know from whence she grew.

## **Tenebrous Steps**

Will this malaise ever cease?
I sit alone, waiting for a call that never comes.
Does she comprehend the pain this puts me through?
I live in hope that I will one day start anew.
She hath her life to share and moreover,
A space to fill with merriment.

Is it normal to wait so long, for another?
To commit your time to them, when they
Have none for you.
I wish upon this sombre sky,
That a star would show me the way.
Instead, each path is full of tenebrous steps,
Like a galleon lost to a ruinous shore.

# Sobriety

As all England sleeps on a winter's night,
An echo creeps closer under the silver light.
A glimmer of something once joyful;
But now, a torment that makes me resentful.
Shadows come from near and far,
Ceasing repose that leaves a single scar.
Lonely and bereft each night that come,
I hear a mocking ghost incessantly hum.
When night turns to morn; having slept not a wink,
This curse remains and my heart shall sink.
Dwelling on years lost to 'Father Time',
I hear caliginous bells eternally chime.
A ruinous crimson adorns my face,
Obsidian tears cascade at pace.
When shall I be free from torturous anxiety?
Will these execrations break my sobriety?

## Desperate Voice

Why must we feel this way?
Why must we suffer in silence?
The unbearable tension between us on this day,
when we could embrace our new alliance.

Why must I wish the day away?
Why must I stare at the hands of a clock?
The intolerable churning, I cannot allay,
when I should break through this mental block.

Oh Love, have I not endured you?
Oh Love, have I not thrown myself at thee?
The ache in my heart is burning true,
when my ship is yearning for your open sea.

Oh Love, have I not proven myself worthy of thee?
Oh Love, have I not shared my reality?
The desperate voice which makes this plea,
when my mind should be free from agony.

## Shouldering Regrets

I never learnt the stratagems required for love; nor the complications that tick away, whether I address them or not.
I never learnt how to express my emotions; nor the implications which would lay before me, whether I address them or not.
I shouldered the weight of grief when I was far too young; the earth's core pulled me close.
I shouldered the weight of fears when I ceased being young; the clouds cumulated and drew me close.
Regrets never leave us, unless we let them go. Whether we send them to the skies; or bury them below.
Regrets never leave us, unless we face them head on. Whether we have a loving companion or go it alone.

## Solace on a Page

I seek solace in the art of writing, as if
It were no longer possible another way.
When this pen drifts over the page,
I am transported to another space and time.
Such a feeling I hope will stay,
But I still hear the whispers of words once forgotten.

When I visit this land of open meadows,
I taste the freedom it means to be me.
It's not a liberation that can be sourced from other shores,
Nor can it be taken by others.
Such a land, only I can see,
May I take each mythical step, once untrodden.

## Knowledge or Hope?

What separates life from death?
Is that knowledge for us to know?
Did the Gods of old bestow?
Should we strive and seek it, until our final breath?
Where shall I find hope?
Am I beholden to the path laid before me?
When the stars have not aligned, do I accept it as a decree?
How can we be free, when we feel there is no scope?

Perhaps it is when the galaxies are united in verse,
And thus, Galileo guides us true.
Perhaps we must wander where the Epicurean Garden grew,
And thus, dispense with superstitions however diverse.
Perhaps we must be candid when cultivating the garden,
And thus, recognise the chains that surround the gate.
Perhaps bearing our souls in love; can remove the hate,
As a bee dances with a flower, allow your resolve to harden.

# The Might of the Pen

A pen is softer with love,
The sword sharper with hate.
The words shine as stars above,
And pierce the armour of fate.

A pen may glide o'er the page,
The sword will shatter bones.
The power of wisdom from a sage,
And tearing into the unknowns.

A word is shielded from decay,
The act withers from memories.
Its presence will last beyond today,
And inflict suffering for centuries.

A word may steel your mind,
The act will break your heart.
It falls from my hand resigned,
And strikes the canvas of art.

## Unquiet Civility

They march, march on unsteady ground,
Armour weighs heavy on shattered cores.
Their swords catch the wind as echoes abound,
'Cling tight my charges, we'll soon hear their roars!'

They march, march towards fortified hell,
Steaks mark the path to death or glory.
Their fatigue is hidden if they remain a shell,
'Quicken the pace, we will end this story!'

They march, march passed fallen brothers,
Blood paints the stones to rouse their anger.
The taste of death seethes and smothers,
'Those cads won't hold this fort much longer!'

They march, march with sweat in their eyes,
Roars are piercing the shallow night.
Their shields gleam bright under moonlit skies,
'Steady men, brace for the fight!'

They march, march in defiant thrall,
Arrows hail down with savage speed.
Their bodies are primed to await the call,
'For England's sake, follow my lead!'

They march, march to deafening cries;
Armour lays beside them, no use has it now.
Their blood is singing so the fallen can rise,
'I will save us from the King, may God allow!'

They march, march no more as one,
Sonorous words are left to the few.
Their strength decays with the rise of the sun,
'From peasants to nobles, if only they knew!'

They march, march as ghosts this day;
From village to temple, they lay within us.
Their heroics will inspire others to say,
'England lives on, it was ever thus.'

## Castle by the Sea

Austere besides the sea; a castle stands,
It holds a home not built with hands.
From whence a King once laid in chains,
All eighteen nights; ice filled his veins.
A fragile voice could be heard from a room,
Where Parliament's guards ensured his doom.
One central pillar that Charles faced in distress;
An inevitable defeat, his captivity would express.

It was here that he felt the walls close in,
Defiance had died, leaving night terrors of sin.
Fed of course as all prisoners had been,
Yet, living without hope cuts the soul within.
This would not be his final place of rest;
Taken to London, with justice put to the test.
Dragged to the gallows after 'guilty' had wrung out,
Bowed to the people; to whom he believed he was devout.

Shielded from nature's despair by Victorian masonry,
Unforgiving armies failed to break its tenacity.
Yet, when Britain's very future was at stake,
Artillery sung skywards with a resolve that could not break.
Men and women; young and old, awaited screeching sounds.
Birds with death on their wings, scorching the sky without bounds.
'Support our lads above us all and give nothing away.'
The mantra that bounced off the castle walls, keeping invaders at bay.

Forts like this withstood the might of oppression far and wide,
'No surrender! No retreat! May each of us stand with pride!'.
For when there was little but blood and grit; amongst this ancient isle,
A love for all that's free; engulfed each Roman mile.
Stood atop the imposing walls, you can sense it even now.
The bravery shown to give all their souls would allow.
And so, when moved to take a trip adown the Solent Way,
Remember the hands of the few, ensured your freedom today.

# The Final Quest

The twilight years of a ship of war,
Hath sheltered saints and sinners alike.
Its life ticks away once left the shore,
The ocean of time is primed to strike.
O' wooden bowels; how you shriek with ardour,
Absorbing sweat and sinew as squires work harder.
Tumultuous waves pull you to and thro,
A skipper's bellows bounce off your heavy timber.
Beleaguered mates sing in the cabins below;
Each ale they swig, makes them limber.
When peril finds you and blood is shed,
Which breaks first; heart or head?

The canons howl on every side,
As smoke engulfs the air around you.
Eyes of each lost soul are open wide,
Oblivion awaits every one of your crew.
O' decaying vessel; how you cry forlorn,
Shattered in the moonlight, each death you mourn.
As one final breath fills the galley,
None remain to mend your frame.
You begin to fall to a sodden valley,

Its loving arms removes your shame.
When the ocean of time lays you to rest,
This bed honours you on your final quest.

## Forbidden Binding

*

Shadowed Lady of my past and present,
How oft I taste your scent so sweet.
When lonely nights are evanescent,
I hear your whispers incessantly repeat.
For if I succumb and hurry to your side,
Disaster lay before each step I ride.

May these words comfort your aching heart,
For I love thee and shall each sojourn hence.
No mayor or magistrate can tear us apart,
Lest you suffer from my expense.
Once the militia move on to another soul;
Together, we shall be exquisitely whole.

\*

My dearest Jack; how I long for thee,
I care not for the burden on my undertaking.
All execrations shall die when we are free,
The future we dream is ours for the taking.
I suspend all thoughts of past indiscretions,
Whispers of love need be our only confessions.

I imagine thy touch on each ghostly eve;
Such powerful emotions, I am powerless to resist.
Aphrodite hath used her threads to weave,
A binding so strong, since first we kissed.
One day soon we shall head for open sea;
Then as now, your faithful Emily.

\*

Exulted have I been since I received you;
Such language warms my soul, dear love.
I feel it like a spell cast so true,
By your Goddess who lay on stars above.
I would be no more were it not for my darling,
Embers of hope are reigniting.

Upon the 'morrow I ride for the place we first met;
I travel hitherto, in hope of romantic success.
There's an inn next door with a room to let,
I pray you shall join me; I must confess.
All that I am; I be but yours,
In everlasting obeisance, my soul endures.

\*

O' dearest Jack! My heart is full of ardour,
Knowing that our rendezvous is set so soon.
Expatiating my love in this way hath become harder,
When I ride for you presently; my guide be the moon.
Father knows nothing of my journey to come,
I leave this life behind; and to devotion succumb.

The stars will lead my carriage to the spot,
Where our eyes first met on a midsummer's day.
In that moment; I felt like time had forgot,
For no others existed; as your smile would convey.
Soteria shall protect me over the nights ahead;
Upon our next kiss, leave the rest unsaid.

\*

The landlord promised these words would reach thee,
For I hath galloped into the night.
With my pursuers close; I had to flee,
And set for the docks before new light.
A local smuggler hath harried me aboard,
I'll await thee where; the future is our life's chord.

\*

O' woe! How lost I felt upon the hearing,
That my wondrous love had left without me.
As hours have passed; I doubt not your disappearing,
Once all 'tis quiet, I shall sail to join thee.
It be but days now; before our life can begin.
Fear not dearest Jack, I shall not give in.

## Song of The Inn

The deepest burrows of yore,
Foundations of warmth were laid.
Lumberjacks brought from the store,
To build in the meadow's shade.
Block by block you were raised,
By village folk's full vigour.
Thy mortar was heavenly praised,
As bricks were set in rigour.

Thou'st opened wide for a furnace,
So flames could rise from the surface.
O' sumptuous flames of the inn;
For when bleak winter drew in,
Thine warmth was the village's harness.

The beams were peaked and porous,
Absorbing the air and ale.
When the villagers sung in chorus,
Your walls would preserve the tale.
Jug to jug were filled,
And emptied just as fast.
When even claret was spilled,
You ne'er winced aghast.

Thou'st opened wide for new folk,
So flames could rise and evoke.
O' sumptuous flames of the inn;
For when bleak winter drew in,
Thine warmth was the village's cloak.

## Ode to Tennyson

When the bells of London told of your death,
Lords and Ladies wept in choral tune.
Collectively tolling as the city held its breath,
Both sides of the river became Camelot's commune.

Your princess sung medleys to her heart's refrain,
The frailty of the fall aged Farringford's walls.
Freshness of the green had begun to wane,
With each tear she dropped; colours bled from the halls.

O' how your scrupulous steps led you to beguile,
All explorers who strolled from Ventnor to Down.
One day your monument would bestride the Isle,
Inspiring creatives from forest to town.

Your knights answered your beckoning call,
Coated in armour bequeathed by thee.
The rigours of the stage that were set in thrall;
From scholar to squire, they danced to your esprit.

O' how your palace was bedecked with flair,
All carvings that depicted a metier so pure.
You ensured the rooms were never bare,
For us to seek our own allure.

When songs were written to charm and indulge,
Tender threads of glee leaped with love.
Effervescent with truths that only a composer can divulge,
They murmured of peace to Apollo above.

Your immortal 'Ulysses' scintillated as cunning epithets often do,
Forming the bond betwixt England and ancient abodes.
Should we lose our patience and struggles ensue,
Endowed to us, is the strength to roam new roads.

O' irascible master; incandescence shook your mind,
To lead us to remember the sacrifice they gave.
As the fog lifted; your words became enshrined,
Ensuring we value a hero, whose life we could not save.

When 'twere prudent for a sonnet to fill thy leaf,
Slender shadows draped idyllic idioms for us to feel.
To be idolised as Pagans once lived their belief,
With divinity in their palm and transience at their heel.

Your life was memorialised for generations thence,
The ferocity of the flame that gave life to us all.

'Twas your blood that ignited your story so tense,
To ensure your remembrance from Somersby to Lurgashall.

O' Lord of poets; in the throes of winter or early spring,
Death is just the beginning, as your radiance lives on.
The heavens shone before you; when you gave the bell a ring.
So, folk for centuries hence; could live in worlds forgone.

# A Friendly Game

The Clubhouse is a temple to all that's English,
From tea and cakes; to pints brewed to nourish.
When we hibernate through winter; we must not forget,
To care for our temple so spring can flourish.

The elements hammer down to push pre-season inside,
From the gale to hail; gelid gloom is betide.
When taking guard seems like months away,
We must defend our crease and more beside.

The mysteries of the game lay behind the door,
So, turning the key allows a novice to explore.
When edging tentatively towards the bar,
Steady your stumps as you hear members roar.

The nuances of a test lay claim to our essence,
So, sharing this with a lover; shows our quintessence.
When lecturing about the play's many acts,
Seek out new ground for your partner's acquiescence.

Excitement reigns supreme as Spring Equinox arrives,
'Let's take a trip aboard a coach, to merry old St. Ives'.
The morning dew sprinkles the outfield blithely,
Warning off certain strokes; on a day a bowler thrives.

Anticipation invades every player's sense,
As they ready themselves for the battle to commence.
The exquisite hush before the start of play,
Sharpens the batsmen's mighty defence.

Adulation blooms amongst the gathering crowd,
For colours are present; that we cheer aloud.
Even if success should not go our way,
Making it to a new season should make us proud.

Merriment reigns supreme as spoils are served aplenty,
From tea and cakes; to pints about to empty.
Each match is different from the one before,
Let's raise a glass; for the game that makes us friendly.

## Winter's Widow

An emptiness fills my soul as the sun starts to rise.
Upon the dawn of Christmas day,
I wake alone; bereft of words to say.
A shadow of purple shields my eyes,
A scarlet tear sits where youth once lay.
Why doth my ashen hands reach for thee?
Pride has left me while I slept,
You are not there when you are meant to be.
I long for days when ne'er I wept.

One single memory repeats in taunting throe;
It speaks to emotions that long hath gone.
Once, they beamed when the sun had shone.
A spectre of joy left long ago,
Each shattered promise; I'm left to dwell upon.
Why can't this soul be made of ice?
When you spoke of my heart being yours,
I became open to love; and now must pay the price.
There can be no festive of light that reassures.

Bedraggled in a heap; I head for the village.
The skies above match my complexion,
Like a pewter vase that blunts my reflection.
Every step takes all of my courage,
Perhaps it's the hope of a fresh direction.
Why doth every sight remind me of thee?
All the towering beeches that bear fruit,
Or chirping robins whom stalk the root.
Yet, there be no branch that shall lead me.

The bells of a church echo in the distance.
Like a siren to a ship; they entice me onwards,
Yet still my head is cowered downwards.
I cannot deny the ringers' persistence,
Striking equal and precise to pull me forwards.
Why doth the chords beat like your quondam heart?
An ageing couple stands atop the path,
They're waiting keenly for the service to start.
My envy of their love is a tormenting wrath.

In place of hymns and religious verbiage,
I must walk on to a setting that sings true,
To face my grief and see this through.
I await your voice with one final message,
Yet, it's stone and flowers that remain in situ.
'Forgive me dearest; for not coming sooner.
I am broken without you; filling my life,
Each passing day feels insanely darker.
Though departed, you shall forever be my adoring wife.

# The Writer all at Sea

Withering under a torrent of gale and rain,
The hut shudders in metronomic hue.
Within, a writer glares in disdain,
For the words he pens no longer sing true.
The beach has turned grey; and his mind has too,
All he can sense is the rattle on the roof.
Once, this setting would ignite a spark.
If success is longevity; then here lies the proof,
But time is the enemy and it strikes in the dark.

Closer and yet closer the clattering persists,
Still not a peep from the panicking scribe.
He glances at the sand; hoping a grain exists,
That sprays inspiration for him to imbibe.
He awaits the tide to bring words to describe,
Or drown the mind with characters to create.
Adorning his coat; he steps into the mist,
When the journey is arduous then open the gate.
New waves await, for the moon to enlist.

# In-between Worlds

She writes of a life once lived,
As if the experiences are closed from her.
A singular acorn that has dropped to the ground,
Left to decay alone; all year round.

She speaks of people; she once knew,
As though their faces are turned away.
A singular stream that has been cut from its source,
Left to dry out; nourishment gone perforce.

There is no feeling to the words she uses,
No link to the senses she had of yore.
A singular stem that has been cut from the rest,
Waiting for death to try its best.

There is no ending to the life she has now,
As if the final curtain is blind to her.
A singular aspect that has dropped to the earth,
Waiting for memory; to bring celestial rebirth.

## Pestilence of Pretence

Surrounded by mourners who wait for the cue,
Their motives unclear behind a villainous veil.
They have all shirked the duty to issue,
An esoteric eulogy that would sharpen this tale.
Exquisitely dressed in gloom upon the moor,
Yet, none carry the grace of a soporific shore.
The quintessence of this 'shower' is vicious to the core;
Their faces taut, in sight of a vexing lore.

'Let's not stand on ceremony', I hear one cry;
An excrescence that befits his looming shadow.
If decorum were a colour; then bleed it dry,
For this murder of crows is pale and shallow.
Even the infrequent tears infect the air,
A pestilence of pretence that disturbs their glare.
The imitation of fealty violates the prayer,
And so, the Reverend contrives to care.

Had I not paid the diggers in advance,
Would any of these plebians have emptied their purse?
With spades at their side; they're unable to glance,
For the scene resembles a pernicious curse.
Splenetic are the coachmen who stand aside,

Maintaining the carriage is their life's only pride.
Watching from afar; my servant be my guide,
To the truth of how I so violently died.



Secreted amongst the throes of my tedious life,
Lay the stones of a soulless existence.
Is it any wonder, the vulture sharpens his knife?
Such a corruption of spirit; cut hope's defence.
'Lay your wreath and leave me in peace!'
This circle of lamentation is merely a caprice,
Platitudes are meaningless; should this haunting never cease.
May all those above me, shed their cruel fleece.

## Sharing the Seasons

Sharing these hopes that once I felt,
Hath become a jaunting journey with no end.
Decaying amongst the leaves where once I knelt,
With stifled roots that cannot mend.
Must I return to paths already trodden?
Any step back will be worn and sodden.

Trying to please to show that I've learned,
Or raise their spirits so festive and free.
Yet, I curse at every opportunity spurned,
When I should be joyous with yuletide glee.
Must I forsake all frightful doubts?
Wake me when floral fragrance begins to sprout.

Rising to expectant chivalrous acts,
Has become onerous; amongst the morning dew.
Leaving a message no longer attracts,
For it ceases to form something new.
Must I change and seek fresh leaves?
Lead me to the garden and pull up my sleeves.

I may thank those who've helped me along,
Or set them at ease in the evenings hence.
Yet, I feel their resentment burning strong,
When I should be glowing with a blissful sense.
Must I sail to lands foreign and exotic?
Wake me when sand and sea are symbiotic.

# Clear the Canvas

When all you can see are empty lanes,
March with pride on England's planes.
When the sky turns white in odious form,
Pick up your brush and paint it warm.
When you've risen late on a day so full,
Breathe slowly; let serenity be your pull.
When howling surrounds you from every side,
Hold on tight and maintain your pride.
When shadows appear which can't be seen,
Allow a supporting cast to intervene.
When bleeding becomes your waking day,
Fight on with a heart that beats away.
When friendships have drifted and some disappear,
Stretch out a branch to those you hold dear.
When words lose their meaning from the ones you love,
Step back and admire the wings of a dove.
When you feel you're in amber or back in red,
Speak out; so the world knows your dread.
When it's easier to stay rooted in one stygian spot,
Draw back the curtains and end this rot.
When voices tell you that all is lost,

Call a friend or stranger, no matter the cost.
When terrors fill your dreams; night after night,
Remember I'm here, to help you shine bright.

## Seeking Commonality

Knocking at the door, you said.
Walking on the silver moor, you said.
Don't go, you plead.
Never change, you plead.

I truly appreciate it, you claimed.
It means so much, you claimed.
I'm lucky to have you, it read.
Thank you for your kindness, it read.

Hold me tight, I said.
Show me the light, I said.
I'm lucky to have you, it read.
Thank you for your kindness, it read.

You make me whole, I claimed.
It fills my soul, I claimed.
I'm lucky to have you, it read.
Thank you for your kindness, it read.

# When Christmas Stopped

I

'We had been here before.'
Lives put on hold with little warning,
Minds left cold with clouds at every turn.
We had ceased to look forward to a new dawning,
Or seek new lessons for us to learn.

'This was different, so different.'
We sacrificed so much in tiring hope,
We gave up touch of those we hold dear.
This was all given so heroes could cope,
Or at least that was the collective fear.

'We had heard them before.'
Lives ignored for lack of funds,
Minds uncared for as they lacked the will.
We had ceased to remember feverish fun,
Or seek new partners to climb the hill.

'This was different, so different.'
We sacrificed blindly for festive delights,
We gave up acting wildly when we had every right.

This was all given so children could see lights,
Or parents give out hugs on Christmas night.


II

'Villages were empty and cities bare.'
Did you walk the streets on an eve?
Or baulk at the beat of silence?
Village greens saw lusciousness leave,
As cities fell away from urban subsidence.

'The high street cried and tradition died.'
When a store lost its way; there was little choice,
When a door closed in our face; nae others would appear.
The highest of Mount Snowdon lost its voice,
The lowest of Stourbridge no longer sung clear.

'Villages were ghostly and cities not there.'
Did you mask your emotions on an early morn?
Or ask your devoted lover for support?
Villages hummed in perpetual mourn,
As cities cawed when ravens fought.

'The high street cried and tradition died.'
When the bars faced a cliff; some tipped over,

When artists couldn't riff; they bowed out from the stage.
The longest of intervals that lacked a composer,
As the shortest sequence murmured with rage.


III

'What were we left with?'
We made do with technology like never before,
We laid plans to 'host' or jump on board.
Organisers formed keys to open the door,
Volunteers gave their hearts for no reward.

'What did we need?'
The scent of cloves mulled over in wine,
As we leant over the pan filled with treats.
We marvelled at the fayre; we deemed divine.
We raced to the chair; to peak at the meats.

'Who were we left with?'
We made do online with our dearest friend,
We laid plans to get on the line with grandparents too.
Organisers became the beacons for light to descend,
Volunteers gave their all so we would make it through.

'What did we need?'
The power of the imagination strengthened our resolve,
As we showed one another that we are ne'er alone.

We gathered in spirit; seeking puzzles to solve.
We danced for the love of it; Yuletide was ours to own.


IV

'I love you with all my heart.'
Did you open a gift that made you feel present?
Or close a rift that had kept you apart?
When the clouds would clear; connections were crescent,
When shrouds disappeared, sensations would start.

'To absent friends, we miss you all.'
For those who ne'er got the chance to grieve,
As farewells were stolen on life's final eve.
You endured all the pain that sorrow could conceive,
You wondered the lane seeking tomorrow's reprieve.

'I love me for surviving this fight'.
Did you open your heart to an appreciation of life,
Or close the book on a haunting strife?
When the clouds were clear; laughter was rife,
When shrouds disappeared, the bubble blunted the knife.

'To absent friends, we miss you all.'
For those whose pages couldn't be read,
As the book was closed; bringing life to a head.
You shall ne'er leave us in the Christmases ahead,
You shall remain the wreath, the wine and the bread.